gs

MW00882903

# How Do Cats Do That?

# by

# Peter Scottsdale

# Table of Contents

# How Do Cats Communicate?

Cats communicate in many ways. They vocalize, use body language, take action, and release scents.

1. *The Vocal Cat*

Cats make three types of sounds.

A. Murmurs

- which includes purrs, trills, and chirrups

B. Meows

- which includes the basic "meow," mews, and calls

C. Aggressive Sounds

- which includes growls, snarls, hisses, yowls, shrieks, and spits.

*Murmurs*

Purring is an ongoing, gentle vibrating sound that indicates a positive state in the cat. However, cats are also known to purr in stressful situations, like when they are seriously injured, in pain, sick or tense. It is believed cats purr when they are content, need a friend, or giving thanks for care, such as when vet treats an injured or sick cat and gets a purr for it.

Kittens learn trilling from their mothers as she will use it to tell her babies to follow her. Adult cats trill in greeting, usually to another feline. A trill sounds like a short purr and meow combined.

Chirrups are meows that roll off the tongue. Mother cats use chirrups to call her young from the nest. It is also used by friendly felines when approaching a human or another cat. Cats make excited chirrups and chatters when watching or stalking prey.

*Meows*

The most known sound cats make is the "meow." Kitties meow mostly for humans and can be plaintive, assertive, welcoming, bold, friendly, attention seeking, complaining or demanding. Sometimes the meow is silent with the feline opening her mouth but nothing comes out.

Mews are soft, early sounds kittens make and are used to get mother's attention.

Calls are made by females in heat and are known as "caterwauling." Males as well make calls when fighting, especially over females during mating.

*Aggressive Sounds*

Growling, hissing, snarling, and spitting are vocalizations cats make when in either defensive or offensive mode. These danger sounds are often combined with body posturing to affect a threat, for instance when a cat puffs up his fur and hisses at a dog that gets too close. When growling, the puss is giving a warning of "back off before you get the claws."

Cats hiss when angry, startled, afraid or hurt. A feline invading another's territory will get hissed and growled at, and if he doesn't leave, he may get attacked.

## 2. *Body Language*

Cats use body language to express a wide range of emotions. To communicate fear or aggression, the cat will arch her back, puff out her fur, and use a sideways position. And to signal relaxation, the cat's eyes will slowly blink or have his eyes half open.

This body language is communicated through the feline's facial expressions, tail, body and coat posturing.

*Posturing*

When cats become aggressive, their back end goes up with stiffened hind legs, tail fur fluffed out, nose pointed forward, and ears flat. Such posture indicates danger, and the cat will attack. This form of feline communication is meant to frighten off an aggressor and prevent an attack. It is a warning.

A scared, defensive feline will make himself smaller, lowering his body to the ground while arching his back and leaning away from the threat.

Cats can show comfort or trust when lying on their back and exposing the belly. However, this may also indicate the cat is about to defend himself with sharp claws and teeth.

Playfulness is indicated with an open mouth with no teeth exposed.

*Ears*

A cat's ears can reveal various states of mind. With ears erect, the feline is focused and alert. Relaxed ears show the cat is calm. Flattened ears happen when the feline is extremely aggressive or defensive.

*Eyes*

Staring communicates a threat or challenge and is an indicator of hierarchy with lower-ranking cats withdrawing from a stare down by a higher-ranking feline. This stare is used often for territory or predatory reasons.

*Tail*

A cat's tail is a great communicator. For instance, a tail swinging from side-to-side in a slow and lazy fashion shows the cat is relaxed. A twitching tail occurs in hunting or when the cat is irritated or displeased and can occur before an attack, playful or otherwise.

When playing, kittens and younger cats will put the base of their tail up high and stiffen the tail except for an upside down u-shape, signaling excitement and even hyperactivity. This tail position can also be seen when chasing other cats or running about by themselves.

Surprised or scared, a cat may erect the fur on its tail and back.

(Also see: "How Do Cats' Tails Work?")

## 3. *Physical*

*Grooming & Other Forms of Affection*

Cats show affection with other cats and some humans by grooming, licking, and kneading. When a feline purrs and kneads at the same time, she is communicating affection and contentment.

A friendly greeting between cats occurs when they touch noses and sniff each other. Bumping heads and cheek rubbing between kitties displays dominance toward a subordinate cat.

A friendly greeting with a human is shown by face rubbing. The feline pushes her face into the person relating affection. The "head-bump" is another way cats reveal positive feelings for a human. Leg rubbing is another form of affection.

As cats rub and push against another cat or a human, they are spreading their scent, which is a form of marking territory.

(Also see: "How Do Cats Show Love?")

*Biting*

Strong biting accompanied by growling, hissing or posturing displays aggression. Light bites show playfulness and affection, especially when combined with purring and kneading.

Another way biting is used by cats to communicate is through mating. The male will bite the scruff of the female's neck, and she will get into the lordosis, revealing she is ready to mate.

(Also see: "How Do Cats Mate?")

## 4. *Smells*

Cats use their own scent to communicate with other cats. By rubbing and head-bumping, kitties use scent glands in their face, tail, paws, and lower back to spread their scent. As well, they use feces, urine, and spraying to leave a message to other cats.

Spraying marks the cat's territory, both indoors and out. Leaving urine and feces is also used to mark a cat's domain.

Additionally, rubbing their scent on objects, like a fence post, marks territory.

Spraying males do the most frequent territory marking. Tomcats spray not only to mark their domain but also to let other toms know the females nearby are his for the mating.

Tomcat spray is a strong smelling marker. Sometimes females will spray, too.

(Also see: "How Do Cats Spray?")

And that's how cats communicate.

# How Do Cats Purr?

When a cat wants to purr, the feline brain will signal the vocal folds to vibrate and produce a purr. Along with the muscles of the larynx, the cat's glottis – the space between the vocal cords – gets larger then smaller quickly. With the glottis repeatedly getting larger and smaller and larger and smaller, the cat's vocal cords separate, and the throat produces a purr.

Purring happens when both exhaling and inhaling. Unlike meowing, which only occurs when the cat exhales.

And that's how cats purr.

# How Do Cats Show Love?

*Ten Ways Cats Show Love*

1. With Purring

A cat's purr can mean several different things. However, when your kitty is near and purring, she is expressing her love.

2. With Rolling

When cats roll around your feet, they are expressing love. With tummy in the air, the cat is greeting and inviting the attention of someone he loves.

3. By Kneading

When your cat kneads against your leg or another part of you, the love comes through.  As kittens, felines would knead their mother's breasts to stimulate milk production.  This behavior continued after weaning to show contentment, relaxation and love.

## 4.  With Gifting

When your furry hunter brings home his prey, he is showing off and offering it to his loved ones, revealing his love for the household.

## 5.  By Raising The Tail

When cats hold their tails straight up with a slight curl at the top, they are giving a love greeting.  Kittens have their tails this way when mom comes close, and then they transferred that to their human mom – you!  Add a twitching tail, and you have complete love.

## 6.  By Rubbing

Yes, cats are spreading their scent by rubbing you, but they are also showing their affection for you.

## 7.  By Talking

A meowing cat typically wants something, like food.  And they show love by meowing.  Only talking to the ones they love.

## 8.  By Grooming

Cats groom others to express love and affection to humans and other animals. By licking you, your cat is caring for a family member.

9. With Cuddles

By curling up on you – perhaps with a nap too – your puss is loving you. Think about it, do you cuddle with people you don't care about? Neither do cats.

10. By Bonking

When your furry friend bumps his head into yours, sometimes followed by rubbing, he is showing love.

And that's how cats show love.

# How Do Cats Jump So High?

Cats' leaping ability is the result of evolution developing strong hindquarters. After catching their prey, early cats needed a place of safety and security to enjoy their catch. Up a tree is the perfect place for cats to eat their meal. So cats adapted and developed powerful leg muscles and flexibility to leap up a tree carrying prey held in their mouths.

Cats can leap up to six times their height. With extremely strong back and leg muscles and a flexible spine, cats can release sudden, powerful bursts of energy.

Felines ready themselves for a high jump by testing the stability of the lower surface with his/her hind legs. When satisfied it's okay, a cat will:

1. Crouch

2. Bend the legs

3. Tighten the body

4. And with a sudden burst, spring upward to a high surface.

And that's how cats jump so high.

# How Do Cats' Tails Work?

Tails play an important part in balance while jumping and righting a cat so she can land on her feet after a fall (also see "How Do Cats Land On Their Feet?").

Felines show emotion and disposition through their tails:

1.  A cat is content and relaxed when she has a curved, S-shaped tail.

2.  A straight up tail with a curved tip shows curiosity and interest.

3.  A kitty is being playful with an erect tail and a small sway.

4.  A swinging tail that hangs reveals impatience and anger.

5.  An annoyed feline curves her tail and twitches the tip.

6.  A low tail tucked between the hind legs indicates submission.

7.  A scared cat will hold his bristly tail down.

8.  A stiff, fluffed out tail indicates anger and the possibility of aggression.

9.  A large puffy, curved tail is a warning of fearful anger and a coming attack.

10.  A feline thrilled to see someone is shown by a tail that stands stiffly up.

11. A cat that flicks his tail is hurling an insult.

And that's how a cat's tail works.

# How Do Cats Use Their Whiskers?

A cat's whiskers are stiff and large hairs that have sensitive roots. With their whiskers, cats can feel objects close to their face. These feelers tell the feline when to blink or close his eyes when something gets too close. Whiskers help detect the direction of a scent on the wind. They also function so the cat can make minor movement corrections, such as helping the eyes and ears concentrate while hunting.

Additionally, cats' whiskers are believed to aid the feline in judging width.

These highly sensitive hairs act as radar for the puss. They can detect the smallest touch or pressure. In areas too dark for even the cat to see, the whiskers guide the feline through and around objects.

In hunting, whiskers protrude and help locate the prey and guide the killing bite.

And that's how cats use their whiskers.

# How Do Cats' Nails Get Sharp?

Cats scratch on rough surfaces to keep their nails in top condition. However, scratching does not sharpen the claws. Rather, when a cat scratches, he is shedding the old outer claw and exposing a new pointed and sharp claw beneath.

And that's how cats' nails get sharp.

# How Do Cats Wash Themselves?

Cats keep themselves clean by grooming their fur. They lick their coat with their rough tongue that contains many papillae, backward facing hooks. The papillae help to clean the feline of dust, dirt, parasites, loose and dead fur, and other debris. For places difficult for the tongue to reach, the cat will lick her paw and rub the area, keeping it clean. You see this when cats wash their face, ears, and head.

Most cats groom themselves about one-third of their waking hours.  By licking themselves, their coat stays clean, soft, and glossy.

And that's how cats keep themselves clean.

# How Do Cats See?

## How Do Cats Eyes Work?

Thanks to their protruding eyes, felines have 285-degree peripheral vision, resulting in a wide angle of sight.

Cats have binocular vision meaning they can overlap images and see the same sight in both eyes. Their field of vision overlaps by 98%, helping the cat determine distance, depth, and size. Their depth perception allows them to see up to 120 feet away.

However, cats have fewer cones than humans and cannot detect motion as well in bright light. The fewer cones impede a cat's ability to see detail.

Resulting from different densities of photoreceptors in their eyes, felines cannot see colors as well as humans. It's

believed cats mainly see red, blue, and yellow.

*How Do Cats See In The Dark?*

Cats see very well in dim light, but our felines cannot see in total darkness. They only need one-sixth the light humans do to see. Felines have a large number of rods – light collecting cells – letting cats see in low light. With wide pupils that let in more light, cats can make their way around and even hunt in the dark.

Additionally, cats have a special layer of mirror-like cells in their eyes behind the retina called tapetum lucidum that are made up of zinc and protein. These are located at the back of the eye and reflect light increasing its intensity, helping the cat to see in darker areas. These cells also make the cat's eyes glow in the dark.

And that's how cats see.

# How Do Cats Identify Their Owners?

Our felines seem to be able to know who we are. We might think its because they see us. However, they do not see the same way we do. Using their vision, it is believed cats recognize us by body language. If we change our body language, like trying to sneak on them, they may not recognize us and avoid us.

Another way cats identify their owners is by the sound of their voice. Even using different pitches and accents, our cats know us.

And, of course, kitties rely on scent to identify humans. When approaching some cats, the feline will stick his nose out to smell you before you get any closer. Cats have an excellent sense of smell and use it to identify many things, like cats, dogs, other animals as well as spray markings of other felines.

So, cats recognize and identify their owners by sight (body language), hearing (voice), and smell (scent).

And that's how cats identify their owners.

# How Do Cats View Their Owners?

Cats view their owners as their mother.

People allow the house cat to insist on affection, attention, security, and warmth just like a mother would.

Humans provide fully edible, ready to eat meals like a mother, where the feline becomes affectionate at mealtime.

People provide shelter and protection from other cats, dogs, and other animals, and cats don't have to compete for territory in their home. These are other ways humans are their mothers.

We talk to cats with a higher tone because cats seem to be more responsive to the higher tone as if they are reacting to their mother.

Many cats will suckle on our clothes and skin often drooling at the same time to stimulate milk flow from her mother to some degree. This suckling is the result of a maternal relationship we have with our cats. We are their mothers.

And that's how cats view their owners.

# How Do Cats Play?

Cats, especially young ones, love to play. Cat play mimics hunting, teaching felines to stalk, pounce, and deliver the killing bite. Play fighting with other kitties, humans, and other animals helps with actual fighting. By play fighting, cats lessen their fear of real combat.

Felines prefer to play with toys resembling prey, such as mouse-shaped toys and strings with feathers attached. Cats like quick moving toys. They will play with non-prey shaped objects, for example, balls and a laser light.
Hunger increases playtime.

## The Kitten At Play:

1. Kittens start to play at three weeks of age. Cats and kittens who do not play are usually lousy hunters and social misfits.

2. Kittens start playing at first by jumping each other, grappling, and rolling over each other. A few weeks later, they will chase, clutch with their front paws, kick their hind legs, and try hunting maneuvers, such as hiding, crouching, stalking, running, and pouncing on their "prey," mostly another kitten.

Kittens' play starts to decline at five months of age, because, some experts say, in the wild their mothers would have put them out on their own.

3. At six to eight weeks, kittens get into mock fights with swatting, chasing, holding, kicking, wrestling, and neck-biting all in the name of fun.

Cats do continue playing long into adulthood.

Older and younger cats will play and participate in mock fights with other cats.

Even the most sedate cat will play every now and then.

And that's how cats play.

# How Do Cats Adapt?

Cats are highly adaptable. Cats' adaptability has made them highly successful. They can survive on different diets and in many living conditions, thriving in many areas of the world, even living in the Antarctica.

This adaptability seems common in both domestic and wild species of cats and is handed down through the generations. For example, in the early 1900s Chicago, cats were used to keep the rat population down in a cold storage warehouse that housed meat the rats would feed on. Many cats died in the cold, but those that survived had kittens with thicker coats and shorter tails to resist the cold. This offspring also became great rat killers, proving the adaptability of the cat.

And that's how cats adapt.

# How Do Cats Fight?

Catfights go down like this:

1. The two cats check each other out with sniffing scent glands in the face.

2. The aggressive one will smell the base of the other one's tail and growl threateningly, and the opponent goes on the defensive.

3. The aggressive cat is ready to attack, and the defensive one crouches low with tail and ears down. Sometimes the aggressor will stop there, as the defensive one will back off.

4. If the opponent challenges a fight will go down.

5. The opponent will adopt a defensive pose by arching his back and turning sideways to look more intimidating. The tail curls up and bristles outward.

6. The aggressor, unafraid, moves in.

7. The opponent crouches down, his ears flatten, and he hisses.

8. The aggressor attacks, and the opponent defends himself claws out and kicking. Kicking, clawing, and biting continue until one slinks or runs off.

9. When a cat turns and runs away from a confrontation, the victor cat will sometimes give chase and attack or may choose to leave the loser cat alone.

And that's how cats fight.

# How Do Cats Protect Themselves?

Cats will adopt different strategies to protect themselves. When threatened, they will arch their back and their fur will stand on end. This is to look bigger and more intimidating to scare away the aggressor. Or the feline may climb up high, like up a tree, to escape trouble. Some will hide in small or hidden places not accessible to bigger, badder creatures. Also, the cat may become violent. With claws and teeth, the scared or cornered feline will attack, sending the attacker fleeing.

And that's how cats protect themselves.

# How Do Cats Hunt?

Cats have two hunting strategies:

1.  The M or mobile hunting strategy that involves moving through fields, grasslands, and forests with all senses in full use with various stops to investigate the immediate area. The M-strategy is effective when hunting rabbits.

2.  The S or the sit-and-wait strategy that involves finding an area where prey frequents and sitting and waiting until prey appears.  This occurs when the cat finds a mouse hole or a run where rodents scurry or below a bird's nest.  The cat

waits undetected until a mouse appears or a bird lands then he pounces.

In recently disturbed areas where rodents are not familiar with escape routes; the cat may choose either the M- or S-type of hunting strategy and take advantage of the prey's confusion with the new area.

Cats only hear rodent sounds when prey is a short distance away. Therefore, cats tend to move about their hunting grounds to pick up the sound rather than staying in one spot.

Cats can hear and determine how far away their prey is. Cats achieve this by being able to independently move their ears by at least 180 degrees.

Cats hunt with patience by staying still and hiding, usually crouching, for long periods until prey is close enough to pounce on. An experienced cat hunter may wait 3 – 4 hours motionless, except for their twitching tail, to pounce on a mouse that comes out of its hole. They usually notice movement in their prey over smell.

Felines find corridors where mice and other small mammals run then they wait until one comes along.

Cats hunt birds by hiding in tall grass or gardens, stalking and crouching until they pounce.

Hunting for cats is a quiet, efficient action relying on stealth and speed to catch their prey.

With blotches, spots, stripes, and different hair lengths, the coat is designed to camouflage the cat as he approaches prey.

When stalking, the cat, with senses functioning highly, spots the prey. He then moves slowly and deliberately and silently toward the prey, sometimes with short bursts of speed and then stops, starts and stops. Cats tend to stalk in this manner when hunting birds. The feline keeps low to the ground with the shoulders and remaining body crouched. When he gets close enough, he sets himself up for the final assault, known as the "lie and wait ambush." With pupils dilated, ears up, whiskers pointed forward, widely spread back paws moving quietly, and rear end wiggling to prepare the muscles and to "fool" their motion sensitive eyes to see still prey more accurately, the cat strikes. With fore claws grasping the victim, the cat bites at the nape of the neck penetrating to dislocate the spine. If the bite is off the mark, doesn't penetrate, or if the prey is too large, the cat may release the prey and pounce again or shake the animal to disorient it and bite the neck again.

With larger and/or well-armed prey, like rats, the hunting feline may attack with their claws until the victim is weak and the nape bite can be delivered. Also, the prey may be held down by one paw as the cat strikes with the nape bite.

When reaching high speeds quickly, the cat's muscles tire fast because of the large amount of energy needed to go that fast. So hunting happens in quick, short attacks. If the puss is unsuccessful in capturing his prey quickly, he gives up rather than running the prey down over a long period.

If a bird flies too low, the feline can leap up and, with claws extended, catch the bird in mid-flight.

While cats do hunt birds, they prefer rodent prey.

Cats mostly hunt at night, dawn, or dusk.

And that's how cats hunt.

# How Do Cats Pee?

## *How Do Newborn Kittens Pee?*

Newly born kittens need their mother's help to pee. She will lick around the kitten's bladder and genitals to stimulate the young one to pee. If a kitten does not pee, it can kill him or her. At about three weeks old, kittens can pee on their own.

## How Do Older Kittens & Adult Cats Pee?

Cats prefer to pee in loose dirt or sand so cat litter is a great alternative to dirt and sand.

When cats pee, they get into the litter box and sniff around and perhaps bury other cats' messes before they go. The feline will squat with hind legs spread outward, tail up in the air, and then he/she will pee downward. Afterwards, the cat will usually bury the pee and leave the litter box, shaking off litter stuck to its paws.

And that's how cats pee.

# How Do Cats Spray?

Mostly adult unfixed males spray to mark their territory, but all adult cats, male and female, fixed and not fixed, can and do spray.

After picking a spot to spray, the cat will turn his backend to the spot and lift his tail. With tail quivering, he will release the spray. Sometimes only a few drops will be deposited or the area could get quite wet. When it's done, the feline will turn around and sniff the wet spot, making sure it is marked, and walk away.

And that's how cats spray.

# How Do Cats Mate?

At puberty, the male kitten has a surge of testosterone from the developing testes beginning the sexual drive and excitability of the emerging tomcat.

At adolescence, the unfixed male may mount a person's arm, cushion, or furniture and masturbate, usually after stroking or excitement – this behavior is usually short-lived.

Early sexual acts may indicate a macho tom is developing, resulting in smelly spraying, indoors and out, roaming for females, and establishing large territories.

Cats keep the sexual drives of their wild ancestors, the African Wild Cat.

Sexual activity for cats is a solitary act, each cat for him or herself.

Areas of the cat's brain, which activate sexual arousal, are close to the same as aggressive behavior arousal.

The tomcat smells are pheromones, which are secreted in a fatty viscous form by bodily glands all over the cat. Urine and feces also distribute pheromones.

A tom will spray more and have a rise in testosterone levels when females are in heat.

A caterwauling tom is usually expressing a threat or warning, not a love song. Toms do this when competing for a queen. Like other animals, the cat can get violent or aggressive when aroused if they are upset or challenged.

Courtship of the cat involves friendly interplay and foreplay with touching, licking, and rubbing and is determined by the willingness of the female.

Females can come into heat as early seven months. Females tend to go into heat for ten-day cycles several times a year. Unfixed females can come into heat every three to six weeks.

When a female calls for a mate, she is said to be in oestrus (heat).

A female in heat yowls, screams, groans, rolls, rubs, and pushes her rear end into the air.

Female Siamese cats will constantly yell when in heat.

A female in heat kept inside can still attract tomcats who howl and fight nearby outside.

The female cat has three sexual cycles per year compared to wild cats having only one, and many domesticated cats are polyoestrous; i.e.: they have continuous mating cycles (or are in heat) until impregnated.

Increasing daylight in late winter and early spring triggers a female's heat cycle, yet indoor cats affected by indoor lighting can increase their sexual cycle to occur throughout the year, even in winter.

Heats last about four to seven days or until impregnated. If the female does not mate, she may go into heat every two weeks or continuously until mated.
If the female in heat does not mate she may wander aimlessly about the home or try to get outdoors to attract a male.

Cats rely on their highly evolved sense of smell to find a mate.

A tomcat can detect a female's mating scent from many miles away downwind and can follow that scent back to the female.

Toms are attracted to the scent of the female in heat. These scents are caused by pheromones released from vaginal discharges and in urine and feces. These pheromones are made to create sexual responses in toms.

Unneutered toms tend to fight, wander, and spray urine even in your home, usually because their hormones drive them.

Tomcats consider any females in their territory to be rightfully theirs. However, other males will pick up her calls and scent when she is in heat, resulting in loud fights over the female that can last for days.

Females show they are receptive to mating three ways:

1.    They roll on their backs in a provocative fashion (wriggling),

2.  May paw frantically at the air,

3.  And call out or wail loudly.

When a male arrives, the female may begin rolling in a more elaborate and lascivious fashion, but reject his advances until she is ready at the right time for impregnation.

When she is ready, she will lie down with her hindquarters raised so she can be mounted.

Cat courtship can be long but the sex act is short.

The male circles the female as she signals her willingness to mate by calling and displaying her intentions. When she is ready, the male grabs the scruff of her neck with his teeth and mounts her. He penetrates her while arching his back and thrusts only one or two times before ejaculating. When he ejaculates, the female cries out piercingly as his barbed penis is withdrawn and rips at her vagina. She may then swipe at him in anger. Older, experienced males will get out of the way as quickly as possible when withdrawing to avoid getting slashed.

The queen will thoroughly wash her vulva after each mating. If a male tries to mate with her as she grooms, she will strike him with claws and teeth. When she is done cleaning, the mating process with the same or different male will begin.

Ovulation in the female does not occur until mating actually happens, so when the eggs are released, the sperm can swim up and penetrate them. The irritation in the vagina causes the eggs to be released from the ovaries in about a day, resulting in the sperm being able to fertilize the eggs for up to 4 – 5 days and ensuring successful mating and conception.

The female needs repeated copulation after ovulation has started to ensure pregnancy, resulting in the queen mating with more than one male. She has more sexual stamina than the toms, and when one male is done, another takes over, leading to her kittens having many fathers.

Mating over and over can occur for four days with the male getting thinner and tired from not eating.

If unfixed females do not copulate, they will have more heats with increased frequency until they are mated. The normal amount of times a female goes into heat is about five times every two years.

Mother cats typically give birth after 62 – 67 days after conception.

Queens can have up to three litters a year.

After mating, the male is off in search of another mate, and the queen is left alone throughout pregnancy, birthing, and raising the kittens.

Fertile males can be sexually active throughout their adult lives although their libido may lessen in old age, but they can still impregnate females into their old age.

And that's how cats mate.

# How Do Cats Give Birth?

Pregnancy typically lasts between 62 and 67 days (9 – 10 weeks).

After three weeks, signs of pregnancy – swelling nipples that change color from white to reddish pink – appear. At the fourth or fifth week, the expectant mother's belly will start to swell. During pregnancy, she will gain 20% - 25% of her normal weight, usually two to four pounds, because she is eating more to feed her growing kittens that will also add weight.

A day or two before labor begins; the mother becomes restless and anxious. She will search for a warm, dark, and private closed in space to give birth.

## Pre-Labor

The mother cat will usually lick her tummy and birthing area repeatedly when she is about to go into labor. She will also lose interest in food and persist with her licking. Her breathing will increase, and she may sit open-mouthed and yowl loudly. She may pace the room as well.

## Labor

When she goes into labor, strong uterine contractions with abdominal contractions occur. Usually within an hour of labor, a small greenish sac comes out of the birthing canal followed by the first kitten with the placenta attached. The placenta will slowly follow each kitten after birth.

## Birth

The birth of each kitten should take 10 – 60 minutes each but can take up to two hours.

Each kitten will emerge wrapped in the amniotic sac, a jelly-like membrane with clear amniotic fluid inside. The mother typically will forcefully lick the sac to remove it from the baby cat and stimulate breathing and circulation. At this time, the mother will bite off the umbilical cord.

## After Birth

The new mother bonds with her kittens by licking and nursing her young. Nursing begins soon after birth, sometimes with other kittens needing to be born.

Nursing stimulates contractions in the mother's uterus resulting in a bloody and/or greenish discharge from her birth canal. She could eat some or all of this afterbirth.

Up to ten days after birth, the mother may expel a bloody fluid. Usually, she will quickly lick up the discharge.

And that's how cats give birth.

# How Do Cats Age?

## *Young Kitten*

After conception, birth takes about 65 days. Kittens are born blind and rely on smell to locate mama's nipples. They tend to feed on the same nipple during nursing until they can see and try other nipples.

Heat receptors in the kitten's nose leather aid the young cat until sight and hearing develop.

Kittens' senses develop at different times:

1. Sense of touch emerges first

2. Taste and smell come forth in their third day

3. Hearing happens a few days later

4. Sight appears at about ten days of age when they open their eyes.

Many kittens are born with blue eyes that change color with time.

Kittens start walking at about 20 days old.

Kittens usually start feeding on their own at three weeks and are weaned from their mother after two months.

Boy kittens are competitive at an early age before developing into toms.

71

It is only during their young days that kittens communicate their needs to another cat. They will express hunger, being cold, and other distresses to their mother until they get older.

Kittens sleep more than adult cats, with newborns sleeping away 90% of their day while older kittens and adults sleep 60% of the time.

## Learning To Hunt

Mother cats that hunt raise kittens that can hunt. With kittens at about a month old, the mother cat will bring home prey to her young to smell and taste. She shows them the swift nape bite to sever the spinal cord while avoiding the rodent's mouth and teeth. Half-dead prey is brought back to the nest for the kittens to handle and kill. After a few misplaced bites and getting bitten by the rodent, the kitten learns to bite safely and effectively.

Kittens raised by mothers who do not hunt will only be able to stalk and pounce –as these are instinctual--but not the learned killing bite. Cats not shown how to hunt by their mothers usually do not learn how to hunt.

Additionally, if the mother brings home dead mice for the kittens to eat, the kitten will learn that mice are food and may leave birds and other animals alone when they hunt on their own.

Kittens will play hunt to practice stalking, pouncing, and catching.

*The Playful Cat*

At three weeks of age, kittens start to play. They play by jumping, grappling, and rolling on top of one another. Later, the young cats will hide, chase, clutch with their front paws and kick with their hind feet their prey – usually another kitten.

After developing for six to eight weeks, play escalates to mock fighting with swatting, holding, wrestling, and neck biting.

Playing continues into adulthood.

## Adapting Kittens

Kittens learn to adapt to their surroundings at an early age. They learn what is a threat and what's not as they grow. Exposure, nurturing by mom, and exploring help the young to adapt and judge situations, good and bad.

## Litter

Mothers train their young to first not go in the nest and then to bury their waste by example. Kittens tend to be litter trained at about six weeks.

## The Older Kitten

Mother cats will wean their kittens at eight weeks so the young cats have to get food on their own. A mother cat will edge her mature kittens out of her territory so they will find their own way.

Between six and eight months of age, kittens reach puberty and grow quickly. Females usually grow to their full weight and height by the time their first sexual cycle occurs.

Cats can take a few years to develop their full coat and coloring.

## The Adult Cat

Cats experience a natural age progression.

Cat Maturity vs. Human Maturity

Cat Year 1  =  Human Year 15

Cat Year 2  =  Human Year 25

Cat Year 3  =  Human Year 29

Cat Year 5  =  Human Year 37

Cat Year 10 = Human Year 57

Cat Year 15 = Human Year 77

Cat Year 20 = Human Year 97

Add four human years for every cat year thereafter.

Cats typically live up to 12 – 15 years, but some may live longer, 21 years and more.

Adult cats go through slight changes as they age. For instance, they will play less, have declining energy, and reduced activity.

Middle-aged cats can experience health issues related to age. One such problem, especially in males, is hypertrophic cardiomyopathy that affects the heart muscle where the walls thicken and the heart enlarges.

## The Older Cat

Cats become senior citizens at nine or ten years and start to show signs of old age. Most senior cats get thinner resulting in prominent bones. Greying of the fur around the mouth and nose can develop.

Because of the insecurity that comes with getting old, some cats will call out in the middle of the night wanting reassurance.

Older cats experience stiffness and may seem unsteady. Jumping high is more difficult or impossible. Hearing loss is not uncommon. And fur can mat in areas where the feline can no longer groom her/himself. And some will have an unkempt appearance.

Heat and cold have a greater effect on the older cat. Furry seniors eat less, drink more water, and sleep more.

Aging cats experience more health problems, such as arthritis, kidney disease, hyperthyroidism, diabetes, and cognitive problems.

And that's how cats age.

# How Do Cats Keep Warm?

Cats keep warm mainly because of their fur. Their fur consists of three fur types, each adding protection from the cold:

1. Down hairs form the bottom coat and are soft, fine and short. They insulate the feline's body, conserving heat.

2. Awn hairs make up the middle coat are medium-length and coarse. These hairs add partial warmth to the cat.

3. Guard hairs form the tough topcoat, adding warmth and water resistance. Keeping dry helps the kitty stay warm.

In the cold, the cat will fluff out her fur, keeping warm air close to her skin.

In colder climates, cats grow longer, thicker coats to stay warm.

And that's how cats stay warm.

# How Do Cats Cool Down?

Cats have few sweat glands so they need to cool down in other ways:

1. One way cats cool down is by grooming. In hot weather or after strenuous activity, like hunting or playing, the feline cools down by evaporation. The saliva left on the fur after licking evaporates taking heat off and away from the cat's body.

2. A feline's fur coat also aids in cooling the kitty down. In warm weather, cats shed fur – less fur equals less heat.

3. When the cat is shedding, blood vessels below the skin surface dilate and expel heat.

4. Also, the feline may pant allowing the saliva on his tongue and in his mouth to evaporate, taking heat away.

And that's how cats cool down.

# How Do Cats Sleep?

Cats tend to sleep 13 – 14 hours a day but can sleep up to 16 – 18 hours a day. They sleep more with age.

Kitties sleep lightly 70% of the time with their muscles not totally relaxed. After several minutes of sleep, cats wake up and may go back to sleep.

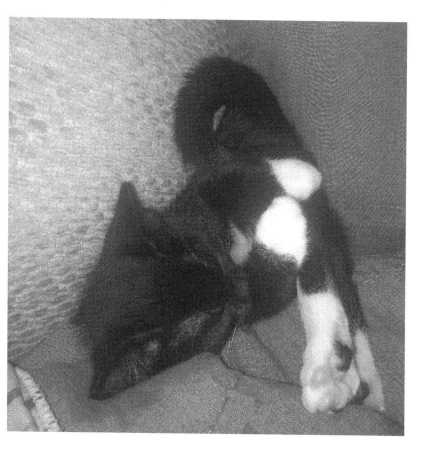

Felines go into deep sleep 30% of the time, and they may experience REM sleep.

Rapid eye movement (REM) sleep causes their closed eyes to move rapidly in quick bursts. Additionally during REM sleep, cats make sounds and move. Their whiskers twitch, ears turn, sleeping positions change, paws and claws move, and they vocalize.

Also our felines dream. During REM sleep, the cat brain experiences electrical activity much like a dreaming human.

And that's how cats sleep.

# How Do Cats Drink Water?

When a cat drinks, she opens her mouth, and her tongue darts out and forms a backward facing ladle. She dips her tongue into the water, filling the ladle. She brings her tongue up and into her mouth where the water is pushed to the back of her throat and swallowed.

And that's how cats drink water.

# How Do Cats Eat?

Cats eat by cutting and shearing their food. Using his front teeth and tongue, the cat will bring food into his mouth. If the cat food is dry and hard, he will crunch it with his back teeth before swallowing it. Soft food is swallowed quickly after entering the mouth. When eating prey, the cat will tear and shear the food using his hind (carnassial) teeth like scissors to break down the meat so it can be swallowed.

And that's how cats eat.

# How Do Cats React To Catnip?

When exposed to catnip, cats love it so much they act like toms when in the vicinity of a female in heat. Catnip excites cats causing ecstasy resulting in rolling, rubbing, and noises of pleasure.

Catnip contains oil that gets cats "high." Catnip is a member of the mint family of plants. The active ingredient in catnip is similar to LSD.

While about 1/3 of cats are not into catnip, usually for genetic reasons, males more than females are susceptible to catnip's effects. Kittens usually don't have an interest in it until about three months of age.

Catnip effects usually last about ten minutes, and the cat will not affected by it for two hours after.

And that's how cats react to catnip.

# How Do Cats Land On Their Feet?

Cats are said to always land on their feet. When a cat falls, he uses his tail to right himself in mid-air. The cat turns his front quarters and headfirst then pulls the hind legs under so that he is facing the ground with feet down. When landing, the feline arches his back to absorb the impact.

And that's how cats land on their feet.

# How Do Cats Find Their Way Home?

One belief is cats use the sun to find their way home after they get lost or their owners move and their cat finds his way back to the old home. Cats know the position of the sun at different times of the day and with trial-and-error find their way home. As the feline gets closer, scent takes over with the kitty smelling his old territory and believing he's home.

What about cats that find their owners after getting lost in a move, even across country? This is called "psychical propensity-trailing" where the feline travels over long distances and varying, even dangerous, terrain to find their family of humans. This is believed by some to be a psychic ability cats have to find their way home.

And that's how cats find their way home.

# How Do Cats Show Pain?

## 1. *Changes In Behavior*

If she become "grumpy" or bad tempered for no apparent reason, she could be hurting.

## 2. *Being Abnormally Aggressive*

A cat in pain is more likely to bite and scratch if he's in pain, especially if the painful area is touch or the cat is moved. Also, if someone gets too near and he's in pain, he may strike or growl.

## 3. *Purring*

Cats usually show pleasure or contentment when they purr. However, purring can occur when the cat is hurting. If your

cat is purring and showing other signs of pain, this may be an indication of discomfort.

## 4. *Excessive Meowing*

Cats that meow a lot more than normal could be hurting. The pain is causing them to cry out.

## 5. *Changes In The Eyes*

Body pain can result in dilated (larger) pupils. Eye pain is revealed with constricted (smaller) pupils. Squinting or excessive blinking can show your cat is having eye pain. Another indicator is a faraway look in the cat's eyes.

## 6. *Changes In Eating & Drinking Habits*

Felines in pain tend to eat and drink less. And if the cat is dropping food and water out of her mouth when eating or drinking is a sign of mouth (tooth) pain.

## 7. *Changes In Grooming*

When your feline stops or decreases her grooming, she is showing hurt or sickness. Excessive grooming in one area indicates pain.

## 8. *Changes In Energy*

Cats in pain can have a decrease in energy. Their activity levels lessons, and they may sleep or lay about more. A decrease in running and jumping could be caused by pain.

## 9. Hiding

A strong indicator of pain is hiding. Your cat may hide for safety's sake when in discomfort. She could hide under beds, cabinets, and couches or in closets. Your kitty's absence reveals a need to protect herself from more pain.

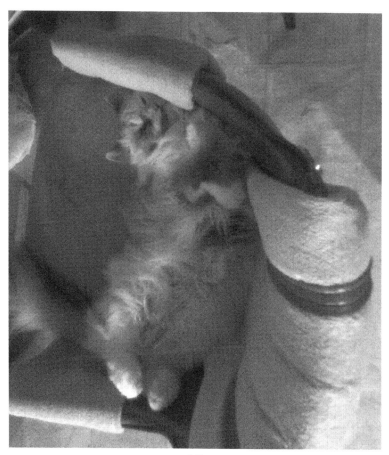

## 10. *Changes In Movement*

A cat will move around less when hurting.  Or he may walk with a limp, have slower mobility, and have difficulty jumping or going up and down stairs.

## 11. *Changes In Litter Box Habits*

Pain can cause cats not to use the litter box even though they're trying to.  Back or hip pain can prevent cats from squatting in their usual position to pee or poop.  This could result in the litter box getting missed and the floor or walls getting messed.  Joint or bone pain could prevent the cat from getting in the litter box, and he may use the floor instead.

## 12. *Swelling*

An area of swelling will usually result in pain.

## 13. *Unusual Sleeping Positions*

Some cats sleep in strange positions.  But if your cat does not normally do that and starts to, hurt could be the cause, especially if she favors one side or the other.  Sleeping in the same position repeatedly where she did not do so before could be a sign of not wanting to sleep in a painful position.

## 14. *Abnormal Body Positions*

A cat hunched up with his feet underneath him and his nose close to the floor could be in agony.  Sitting or lying in unusual positions or walking strangely, like having a hunch, are indictors of pain.

## 15. *Changes In Breathing*

If her breathing becomes faster and shallower, she could be in discomfort. Panting is also a sign. Cats use their abdominal and chest muscles to breathe so changes in those muscles resulting in breathing changes may indicate pain.

## 16. *Changes In Pulse & Heart Rate*

Increased pulse or heart rate could be a sign of a hurting cat. Rates tend to increase when the painful area is touched or moved.

And that's how cats show pain.

<u>NOTE: If your cat shows signs of pain, get him/her to the veterinarian as soon as possible. It could mean your cat's life.</u>

# How Do Cats Get Worms?

Cats can get worms in several ways:

1. Immature fleas eat worm eggs then the grown fleas get on the cat. While grooming, the feline will lick the fleas off his fur and swallow them, infecting the cat with worms.

2. A mother cat infected with worms can pass the worms to her young through her milk.

3. Cats can also get worms from eating prey. If the prey in infected with worms, eating his catch can infect the hunting feline with those worms.

4. If a cat eats or licks an infected cat's feces, the worms can get passed onto him.

And that's how cats get worms.

# How Do Cats Get Ringworm?

Cats get ringworm from other cats or animals. This can happen through direct contact by fighting, licking or other physical contact.

Ringworm spores can live in the environment (i.e.: outside a host) for more than a year. Therefore, cats can get ringworm from skin cells or hairs from infected animals that are left behind in bedding, carpeting, dishes or just about anything a cat has exposure to.

And that's how cats get ringworm.

# How Do Cats Get Fleas & Ticks?

## *In Your Yard*

If you allow your feline outside, he becomes susceptible to flea and tick infestation. Fleas and ticks can occupy your yard, where your cat loves to hang out. These parasites can come into your yard by other animals like feral cats, dogs, raccoons, squirrels, and other small rodents. Any animal that carries fleas and ticks can transfer these bloodsuckers to your cat.

## *Roaming*

Cats that venture into tall grass increase their chances of getting fleas and ticks. These parasites like to climb up a blade of tall grass and attach themselves to passing animals, including cats.

## *At Home*

Cats sitting in open windows can result in an infestation, as the bug only needs to crawl onto your waiting feline. And sometimes screens don't keep them all out.

## *People*

Humans that venture into tall grass and the wilderness can bring fleas and ticks into your home where they will find your cat and begin feeding.

## At Any Time

Whenever the cat is going on a trip out of the home - a visit to the vet, for instance – has the possibility of catching fleas and ticks. Because these parasites can crawl, they can move onto any cat at any time.

And that's how cats get fleas and ticks.

# How Do Cats Get Ear Mites?

Cats, especially kittens, can get ear mites that look like bumps or dirt on the interior of the ears. These highly contagious pests are usually passed from cat to cat.

Dogs can also pass ear mites to cats. In fact, any physical contact with these parasites on another animal, like rabbits or other rodents, can cause an ear infestation.

Outdoor cats are more likely to get ear mites as they have more contact with other animals.

And that's how cats get ear mites.

# Thank You

Thank you for buying and reading this book and for trusting me to inform and entertain you. I hope you'll consider writing a blurb about "How Do Cats Do That?" on Amazon in the book listing's review section. It would be a huge honor if you did! And very much appreciated!

Best wishes always,

Peter

# About The Author

A cat lover from an early age, Peter Scottsdale wrote his first cat tale, "The Cat and the Dog," in a grade three creative writing exercise – the story of a cat and a dog lost in the woods, and the police shooting the dog for some reason. Peter drew inspiration for the story from Disney's *The Incredible Journey*.

Inspired by such books as Hardy Boys Mysteries, Marvel Comics and *Mythology* by Edith Hamilton, Scottsdale wrote several published short stories with his grade nine English teacher.

Then life happened. Scottsdale stopped writing, only scribbling bits of story every so often. A family came along which turned into single parenthood. He raised his kids and wrote here-and-there.

Throughout his life, cats have been a welcome and influencing presence. From Tia (a Siamese) to Booties (a Tabby with White) to Rusty (an orange boy with little ears) to Sam the Siamese, Peter has loved all his felines (and still does). He's loved all his cats so much so he started to write about them. They have inspired and delighted him to create cat stories and to find feline facts for his books.

Cat lover turned author, Peter Scottsdale published his first book, *365 Fascinating Facts You Didn't Know About Your Cat,* in 2012. He followed that with "The Christmas Cat" and "The Christmas Cat 2." Recently he released *How Do Cats Do That?* on Amazon and will publish *The Wonder of Cats* in Fall, 2016 and "The Christmas Cat 3" for the 2016 holiday season, also on Amazon.

An English Major, Scottsdale graduated from Medicine Hat College with an Associate of Arts Diploma in 1995. He continues to research our furry felines and write cat fiction and non-fiction and hopes fellow kitty-cat people will enjoy his work.

Currently, he resides in Medicine Hat, AB with his two cats: Tanzy (the feisty feline) and Alley (the mischief maker).

## Check out other books by Peter Scottsdale on Amazon.

60244625R00064

Made in the USA
Charleston, SC
27 August 2016